The Playground Queen

Written by Casey N. Morris, Ph.D.
& Illustrated by Jasmine T. Mills

For my daughter, Kylah Charlie, who inspires me to inspire others.

What's up, my fellow young Kings and Queens? My name is Kya and I'm going to tell you about my first day as Queen of the Playground.

"Wake up, Kya. It's time to get ready," I heard Mommy calling.

I jumped out of bed, gave Mommy
a big hug and headed to the bathroom.

In the bathroom, I climbed up on my stepping stool so I could see my wild morning curls in the mirror as I brushed my teeth.

"Can you do my favorite hair style?" I asked Mommy.

She smiled and softly touched my chin. "Of course, my young beautiful queen."

After eating a bowl of oatmeal and fruit, Mommy asked,
"Are you ready for your first day as a first grader?"

I shrugged with a crooked smile and said, "I think so."

I was sooo nervous for my first day at school, but I knew I would see Neo, my friend from kindergarten. So at least I would have one friend in the first grade.

You see, last year in Ms. Johnson's Kindergarten class, Neo and I stayed online after class every day to talk about how excited we were to go back to school and play at recess together.

We became best friends.

Mommy dropped me off at my classroom and handed me my hat, my lucky hat.

"Wear it like a crown, young queen," she said.

Mommy reached out her fist to give me a fist bump.

"I love you, Mommy," I said, and then I made my way to class. My mommy didn't know that I wore my lucky hat whenever I felt shy or nervous.

I walked up to my class door, took a big gulp, and opened it.
I slowly poked my head in my new classroom.

My new teacher, Mr. Brown said, "Welcome to class. What's your name?"

I slouched my shoulders timidly and lifted my sweaty hand to wave. "Kya."

My teacher said, "Hi Kya. Go ahead and find a seat."

I looked around to find Neo. I spotted him and was thrilled to have seen my friend, but that feeling suddenly disappeared when I saw he was sitting next to someone else. He didn't even say hello.

I found a seat away from everyone else and slouched down.

Then I heard a voice say, "Hey, come sit over here with us." I turned around and saw a curly head, just like mine. I smiled and walked over.

Ring! Ring! Ring! The bell rang. It was time to go to recess. This year, because I was a first grader, I would be on the big kid playground. Even though it was big, I knew I would be fine because Neo and I had talked about playing at recess online last year.

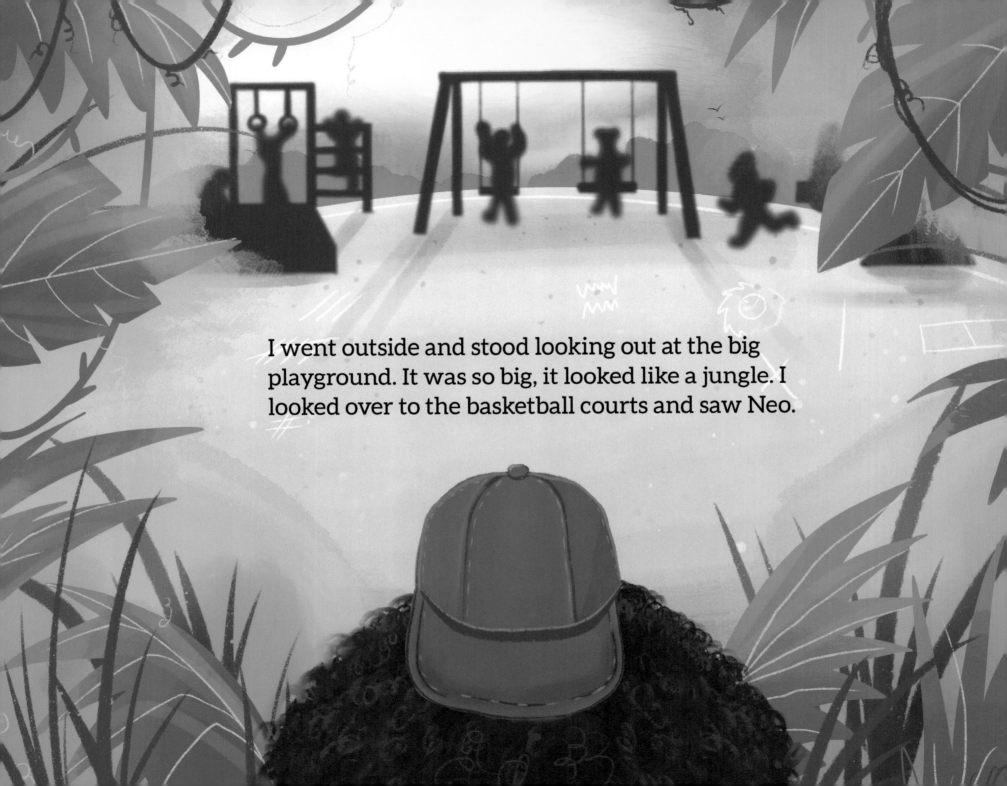

I went outside and stood looking out at the big playground. It was so big, it looked like a jungle. I looked over to the basketball courts and saw Neo.

I stood on my tippy toes to wave so he could see me, but he didn't wave back. I sat down and wrapped my arms around my knees. I felt so sad because Neo didn't want to play with me.

"Hey, Kya," said a voice. "Remember me, Malik, from class? Do you want to play with us?"

I smiled and grabbed his hand as he helped me up.

Malik had a big group of friends. We played all recess long!

We dribbled our way to the basketball courts first. Malik couldn't shoot as good as me, but I let him score a couple of baskets. I counted, "3-2-1." Swish. "That's game!"

We tethered our way to the tether ball pole. It was my first-time at tether ball but my new friends taught me how to play. Around and around and around the ball went.

We hopped to the hopscotch area and put a foot in every square and sang, "One foot, one foot, two feet, one."

Malik shouted, "First one to the grass is at the top of the pyramid."

I ran and ran and ran and made it there first!

I would get to be on the top of the pyramid with all my friends holding me up.

Just as I made my way to start climbing, I saw Neo slowly walking towards us with his head down.

I stuck my hand out just like Malik did to me when I was sitting by myself and said, "You can be a part of this pyramid too."

I climbed to the top of the pyramid of friends and took my hat off. Then I spread my arms out wide, feeling the wind blow around me.

For the first time, I felt like I was the Queen of the Playground!

Author's Note

As a mother who truly believes that representation matters for our young children, and with a daughter who loves to read books, I try to fill my 5-year old's bookshelf with books that demonstrate my beliefs. However, one message I think we are missing is the reality that we still have so much more work to do as a nation before we reach an equally received feeling of equality, inclusivity and diversity, particularly in our schools.

I truly understand the beauty of children's books and how they provide the ability to creatively paint a picture of the imaginative future, but I also love the idea of painting a picture of the beauty of what actually presently exists. The message of "The Playground Queen" teaches our young children the reality that they may experience some form of rejection within their peer group. It teaches them to lean on people in their community to uplift them, and lastly, it teaches the importance of forgiveness.

In our home, we practice Kwanzaa each year. One of the principles of Kwanzaa is Umoja or unity, which means, to strive for and to maintain unity in the family, community, nation, and race. Kya felt rejected by Neo, who ignored her when she returned to school. She felt alone and lost initially but was uplifted by Malik and other kids in her community. Her community empowered her to feel like she was a playground Queen, as exhibited in the strength she sees in her mother. That feeling of empowerment and confidence that Kya's community helped Kya realize, allowed her to forgive Neo and welcome him with open arms when he recognized his mistake of not acknowledging her.

Overcoming. Community. Empowerment. Forgiveness. Togetherness. Allyship.

CPSIA information can be obtained
at www.ICGtesting.com
Printed in the USA
BVHW052150250521
608093BV00012B/322